There Are 3 Ways For You And Your Group To Earn Financial Rewards And Warren Buffett Stock

1) Earn Stock, Cash And Prizes By Attending Live In Person Or Online Classes

2) Earn Warren Buffett Stock Complete "Share The Wealth And Win" And "Earn While You Learn" Courses

3) Earn Stock, Cash And Prizes By Giving Away Free Memberships To SuccessAndMoneyFoundation.org

Groups Can Earn
Cash And Prizes By

1) Having Their Group Attend Live In Person Or Online Classes

2) Having Their Group Complete "Share The Wealth And Win" Courses

3) Having Their Group "Share the Wealth" By Giving Away Free Memberships To SuccessAndMoneyFoundation.org

A Special Thanks To These Supporters That Helped Financially, So That This Book And Courses Could Be Printed and Delivered At A Low or No Cost to The Students and Organizations

Money Angels
The Painter Family And Foundation $3,000,000
Greg Warnock $15,000
Taz and Tammi Murray $5,000
Andrew Smith, Keith Richenbacher, Justin Bauer $1,000

The Success And Money Foundation is Supported by
Best Selling Authors, Educators and Entrepreneurs

Woodbury Private Equity	WoodburyCorp.com
Mercato Private Equity	MercatoPartners.com
R&R BBQ	RandRBBQ.com
Panda Express	PandaExpress.com
Traeger Grills	Traeger.com
DOMO	Domo.com
Utah Community Credit Union	UCCU.com
Yoli	Yoli.com
Vivint	vivint.com

A Special Thanks to Robert Allen, Mark Victor Hansen, Jeremy Andrus, Carine Clark, Ethan, Jacob and Josh and many more

Founders

Tom & LaDawn
Painter

This Book Is Dedicated To My Family

Jim And Zoma Painter
My Parents Taught Us How To
Be Compassionate Capitalist By Example

My Wife
LaDawn, The Love Of My Life
Thanks for Riding With Me on the Roller Coaster of Life

My Children and Grandchildren
You Are a Miracle

Thanks To My Friends, Mentors and Influencers
My Brothers and Sisters
Boyd And Merlene Ivie

Robert Allen
Zelpha And Fenton Broadhead
Dan Kostanko, Ray Russell
Nick Koon, John Childers, Wade Cook
Jan Stephan, Steve Carlson, Sharm Smith,
Paul Rimington, Kurt Mortensen And Mark Victor Hansen

To All The
Success And Money Foundation Students
Thank You For Sharing The Wealth Of Free
Success And Money Classes

If You Would Like To Help Us Share The Wealth Of Free
Success And Money Classes For Anyone, Anywhere

Please Email Me TPainter96@gmail.com

Thanks Tom Painter, Founder

Author: Thomas R. Painter
Book Cover Artwork: Joshua Maverick C. Ledesma
Title: 5 (DETAILED) Success And Money Steps To Financial
Freedom
Subtitle: Your Playbook For A Successful Life
Category: Business And Money

For More Information, Visit:
SuccessAndMoneyFoundation.Org
SuccessAndMoneyFoundation@gmail.com
Tpainter96@gmail.com **(Tom Painter)**

Disclaimer:
The Information Provided In This Book Is For Educational Purposes
Only. It Is Not Intended To Be A Source Of Financial Or Legal
Advice. Making Adjustments To A Financial Strategy Or Plan
Should Only Be Undertaken After Consulting With A Professional.

Take The Pre-Quiz Then Read The Book Then Take The Post Quiz At The End Of The Book

1	**How much would you have if you put a $1 a day under your mattress for 66 years?** $24,090 or $41,458
2	**How much would you have if you invested a dollar a day at 3% for 66 years?** $38,686 or $75,736
3	**How much would you have if you invested a dollar a day at a 10% rate of return for 66 years?** $2,607,064 or $6,533,598
4	**How much would you owe if you charge a dollar a day on your credit card at 21% interest for 66 years?** $16,887,660 or $1,611,877,660
5	**If you used a credit card to buy a computer for $1,000 with 10 years of payments, How much would you pay in total?** $1,300 or $2,374
6	**With $1,000 in debt, After making payments for 4 years, How much do you still owe?** $325 or $771
7	**What is the Dow Stock Market Index?** 100 Companies from different industries or 30 Companies from different industries
8	**What is the S&P Stock Index?** 500 of the largest companies in America or 1,000 of the largest companies in America
9	**True of False, The S&P Stock Market Index makes more money than most professionally managed mutual funds?** True or False
10	**Berkshire Hathaway is a stock that is managed by Warren Buffett's team, over time, does it make more money that the S&P Stock index?** True or False

10 Pre-Quiz Answers

1	How much would you have if you put a $1 a day under your mattress for 66 years? $24,090
2	How much would you have if you invested a dollar a day at 3% for 66 years? $75,736
3	How much would you have if you invested a dollar a day at a 10% rate of return for 66 years? $2,607,064
4	How much would you owe if you charge a dollar a day on your credit card at 21% interest for 66 years? $1,611,877,660
5	If you used a credit card to buy a computer for $1,000 with 10 years of payments, How much would you pay in total? $2,374
6	With $1,000 in debt, After making payments for 4 years, How much do you still owe? $771
7	What is the Dow Stock Market Index? 30 Companies from different industries
8	What is the S&P Stock Index? 500 of the largest companies in America
9	True of False, The S&P Stock Market Index makes more money than most professionally managed mutual funds? True
10	Berkshire Hathaway is a stock that is managed by Warren Buffett's team, over time, does it make more money that the S&P Stock index? True
	How Many Questions Did You Get Right?

TABLE OF CONTENTS

TABLE OF CONTENTS
(Continued)

Step 2: Separate Your Money

Step 3: Give To Individuals, Church And Charity

Step 4: Automatically Invest

TABLE OF CONTENTS
(Continued)

Step 5: Save And Spend

TABLE OF CONTENTS
(Continued)

Putting It All Together

Learn, Earn And Return

The Goal Of This Book

Is To Help

YOU And YOUR

Family & Friends

Live A Better Life

INTRODUCTION

SuccessAndMoney Foundation.Org

For A FREE Membership
SuccessAndMoneyFoundation.org

SuccessAndMoneyFoundation.org

Purpose

Is To Help You And Your Family Have A Better Life

By Providing

FREE

Success And Money Classes To Anyone Anywhere

We Have 3 Missions

Mission #1

Provide Financial Rewards To Students When They Attend Online Classes And Share With Others

Rewards Are To Be Added To Their Investment Account

Mission #2

Provide Donations And An Educational Platform
For
Schools, Churches, Charities, Groups And Teams

Mission #3

Improve People's Lives And Help Those In Need

<u>Our Impact</u>

The Foundation Has Over 12,000 Students

From

80 Countries That Have Attended

Over

150,000 Hours Of Online Classes

The Foundation Has Sent Out Over

30,000

Financial Rewards

To Thousands of Students All Over The World

The Foundation Was Created Because

You

Didn't Attend Classes About Success And Money In School

There Are 3 Ways To Earn Financial Rewards

1) Attend Live Online Classes

2) Complete "Earn While You Learn Courses"

3) Share The Wealth Of Free Success And Money Classes To Family And Friends

The SuccessAndMoneyFoundation.Org

Has Hundreds Of Classes On Success And Money

The Foundation Is Supported By

Best Selling Authors, Educators And Entrepreneurs

Here Are Some Of The

FREE

Online Classes, Books And Downloads

For A FREE Membership
SuccessAndMoneyFoundation.org

FREE Success Classes By

Steve Jobs
Denzel Washington
Admiral McRaven
Arnold Schwarzenegger
Jim Carrey
Matthew McConaughey
Top 10 Epic Motivational Speeches
1 Hour To Change Forever
Excellence
Buffett And Gates Greatest Advice

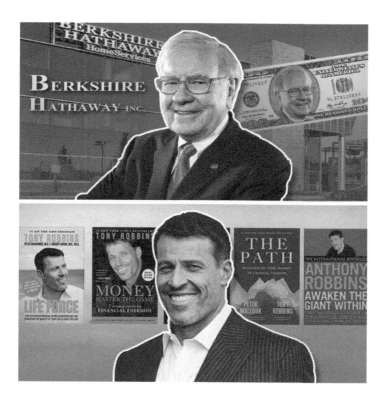

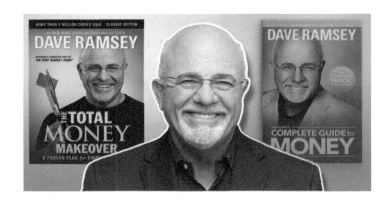

Warren Buffett
Tony Robbins
Dave Ramsey
Elon Musk
Bill Gates
Warren Buffett
Robert Kiyosaki
Oprah
Gail Miller
Steve Young
Walt Disney
Bob Circosta
Cindy Cashman
Dave Anderson

FREE Entrepreneur Secrets By

Ed McMahon
Janet Switzer
Joe Polish
Larry Pino

Larry Williams
Lorrie Morgan
Michael Gerber
Paul Hartunian
Tom Hopkins
Vic Conant
Wyland

FREE STEM
Science, Technology, Engineering And Math

Jeremy Andrus
Mark Zuckerberg
Tim Cook
Mitt Romney And Steve Balmer
Ryan Smith
Carine Clark

FREE Success And Motivational Courses

Millionaire Psychology
Empower Yourself
Inner Success And Wealth

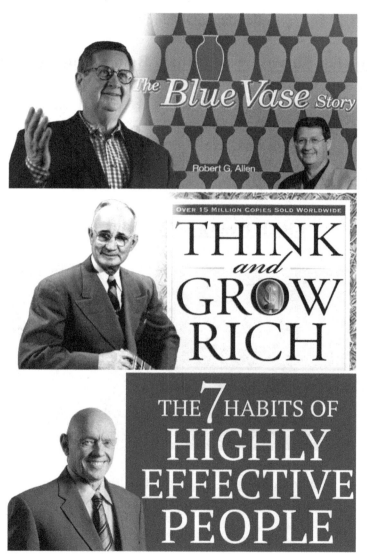

Start Your Day With Power
The Blue Vase Story
4 Maps Of Successful People

Think And Grow Rich
7 Habits Of Highly Effective People
The Magic Of Thinking Big

FREE Success And Money Books And Courses

Dale Carnegie - How To Win Friends And Influence People
The Psychology Of Money
Think And Grow Rich: The Lost Secret
Thank And Grow Rich: Summary
11 Books That Made Me Millions

FREE Health Is Wealth Classes

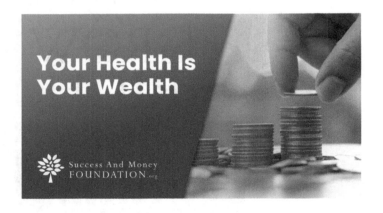

Werner Berger - Living A Healthy Lifestyle
Werner Berger - How I Climbed Mount Everest

FREE Personal Finance Classes

5 Steps To Financial Freedom
60 Day Money Miracle
Young Investors Society Finance Lessons

FREE Small Business Classes

Stephen and Bette Gibson

Michael Gerber - The E Myth
Jay Abraham - Money Making Secrets Of A Marketing Genius
Stephen Gibson - Creating Family Prosperity
Brandon Barnum - Making Money With Referrals
Robert Kiyosaki - Make Money With Direct Selling And MLM
Darren Falter - How To Pick A Network Marketing Company

FREE Money Classes

Ray Dalio - How The Economic Machine Works
Robert Allen - Multiple Streams Of Income
Thomas Painter - Wealth With Low Risk

Robert Allen & Mark Victor Hanse - One Minute Millionaire
Robert Allen & Mark Victor Hanse - Cracking The Millionaire Code
Robert Allen - Multiple Streams Of Internet Income
JJ Childers - Escape
Kurt Mortensen - Crypto And Blockchain 101

<u>FREE Make Money With Sales</u>

10 Sales Techniques That Will Make You Rich

<u>FREE Make Money With Real Estate</u>

Robert Allen - The Road To Wealth
Robert Allen - The Real Estate Launch
Mark Haroldsen - Wake Up The Financial Genius Inside You

FREE STEM
(Science, Technology, Engineering And Math)

Building Your First Website
Building Websites With WordPress
Html And CSS Courses
Learn How To Code

FREE Success Books

Tom Painter - 7 Success And Money Steps To Financial Freedom
Tom Painter - 101 Success And Money Book Summaries
Tom Painter - 501 Success And Money Quotes
Tom Painter - 1001 Success And Money Secrets
Tom Painter - Success And Money For Kids And Teens
Tom Painter - Success And Money For Adults

Robert Allen - Four Maps Of Happy Successful People

Napoleon Hill - Think and Grow Rich
Russell Conwell - Acres of Diamonds

Library Classics
Ultimate Success Library

Jim Painter and the Class Of 1947
If I Could Do It Over Again, I Would …

Mark Victor Hansen - Ask!
Mark Victor Hansen - Recipes For Success
Mark Victor Hansen - You Have A Book In You

FREE Money Books

Stephen Gibson - Creating Family Prosperity

Mark Haroldsen - Wake Up The Financial Genius Inside You
Mark Haroldsen - Next Step
Wake Up The Financial Genius Inside You

Ross Jardine - The 60 Day Money Miracle
Robert Allen - Multiple Streams Of Income

Robert Allen - The Challenge/Road To Wealth

John Lee - Secrets To Winning With Failed Real Estate Deals

Brandon Barnum - Raving Referrals

eBay Riches
Amazon Riches

JJ Childers - Real Wealth Without Risk

<u>FREE Downloads</u>

Money Made Easy Playbook
Money Made Easy Money Trackers
Manage Your Money On One Piece Of Paper-Cashflow Trackers
Million Dollar Bill
Money Made Easy Play Money And Cash Cards
Five Steps, Wealth Formula And 25 Rules Of Small Business
Real Estate Bargain Finder
Property Scoring System
Find It, Fund It, Farm It
The Miracle Of Tithing
How To Make $24,000 In 24 Hours On The Internet
Nothing Down Real Estate Techniques
Zero To $1,000,000 On $49 A Month

FREE Success Quotes By

Robert Allen And Mark Victor Hansen

FREE Success Summaries

Jeff Bezos
Warren Buffett
Dave Ramsey
Robert Kiyosaki
Oprah
Matthew McConaughey
Jim Carrey
Arnold Schwarzenegger
Steve Jobs

Next Step Resources
Young Investors Society
Self Reliance Help
Pathway
Personal Finance
Marriage And Family Resources

For A FREE Membership
SuccessAndMoneyFoundation.org

1

The Day I Discovered

My Purpose

Was

The Day I Almost Died

My life changed in the summer of 1994

At the age of 34, I had a heart attack

As they were wheeling me into the operating room

I looked over at my wife and wondered if I was coming back,

and

If I didn't come back, who was going to take care of my 2 special needs children

I was lucky, 1/3 of the people who have a heart attack die,

In the hospital I made a vow to take better care of myself and to create systems to take care of my 2 special needs children

Our son had been diagnosed with autism, 30 years ago, there were very few programs

We found one at UCLA, that was $40,000 a year, plus we would have to relocate to Los Angeles

$40,000 back then is equivalent to $160,000 today

We just didn't have the money

I spoke with my parents, family and friends and then I got some

Wonderful advice from the famous author, Robert Allen

He was the author of Nothing Down, Creating Wealth and Multiple Streams of Income

Roberts advice was, "Tom, figure out how to make so much money, that you can put your son in whatever program you want and never regret it

LaDawn and I went to work, we fixed up real estate, bought long term rentals, started multiple small businesses and started investing

Flash forward to today

Our special needs children are taken care of

When I turned 60, I knew it was time to share what I had learned with others

So, LaDawn and I created a non profit educational foundation and donated

$3,000,000

of our real estate and Berkshire Hathaway stock

The Foundations Purpose is

To help you and your family have a better life

By

Providing

FREE

Success and Money Classes

To anyone anywhere

So far, we have over 12,000 students from all over the world that have attended over 150,000 hours of online classes

The Foundation has given out over 35,000 small financial rewards to student for attending class and sharing with others

We know of 3,600 students that have started saving and investing, because we have sent them our Warren Buffett, Berkshire Hathaway Stock

In addition

The foundation has supplied over 150,000 eyeglasses, meal or gallons of clean water

As the founders of the Success And Money Foundation

We invite you to join us and

Share the Wealth of FREE Success and Money Classes

By sharing the website

SuccessAndMoneyFoundation.org

And

After you have signed up for your own FREE Membership

Share you personal link with others

Make A Difference, Make It Happen, Every Life is Precious

2

Bucket List First

Then

5

Steps to Financial Freedom

If you have a big enough WHY, You will figure out a HOW

What is a bucket list?

It's all the things you want to do before you die

So lets get creative, doodle, play, dream and plan

We use a system called mind mapping, some people call it a web

We use this system for all kind of things

Let me teach you how it works

You start with a center circle, which is the Main Idea
Then outside circles, which are the Sub Idea
Then outside boxes for Detailed Ideas
Then more boxes for Sub Details

This allows you to concentrate on one circle at a time

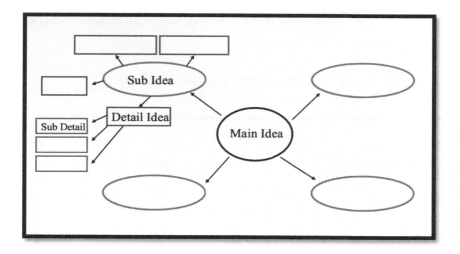

What are you dream?
What charities would you would like to help?
What are the fun things you've done with your family?
What would your house look like?
What toys would you buy, Cars etc?
What are the experiences you would like your children to have?
What do you want your children to grow into?

"Good parents give their children good memories bad parents give their children bad memories" Robert Allen

"The only way to get what you want out of life is to help others get what they want out of life" Zig Ziglar

To teach you about mind mapping

Let's use world travel as an example

I'm going to show you some of my photos, not to impress you but to impress upon you that you can do it

What are the Wonders of the World you would like to see

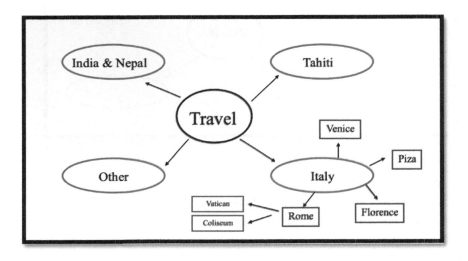

India and Nepal Taj Mahal, India

Nepal, Mt. Everest by helicopter

Tahiti

Rome, Coliseum and Vatican

Charity, Helping women start small business

Taking a group of special needs kids to Disneyland

Use this system to brainstorm and then create action plans to accomplish your dreams

 The great thing about a mind mapping

Is you can use it for all kinds of things

I use in the mornings to determine all things I'd like to get done

After I do the mind map, I number them in order of importance

1, 2, 3, 4 and 5

I attack the 1s and delegate the 4s and 5s

3

5

Steps To
Financial Freedom

5
Success And Money
Steps to Financial Freedom

1. Make More Money

2. Separate Your Money

3.
Give to Church
& Charity

4.
AUTOMATICALLY
Invest

5.
Save &
Spend

4

Make More Money With Your Job

I have some good news, each of you will make, manage and spend

Between $1 million and $10 million dollars

The bad news is that, most people will die broke and in debt

The way you become financially independent is to

1. Solve Bigger Problems
2. Add More Value
3. Study Successful People

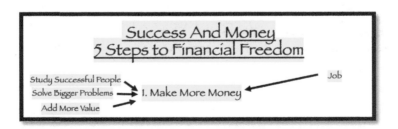

The Success And Money Foundation Offers

<u>FREE Make More Money With Your Job Classes</u>

Salary Negotiation
How To Ask For A Raise
Know Your Worth, Then Ask For It
How To Find Your Passion And Make It Your Job
How To Find A Job
How To Find A Better Paying Job
Take A Harder Job To Make More Money

Additional Free Courses
SuccessAndMoneyFoundation.Org/Courses

5

Make More Money With Your Small Business

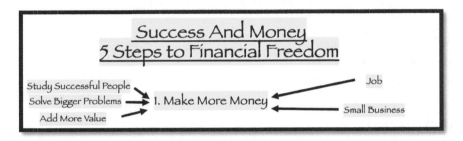

"Some People Make So Much Money From Their Small Business, Investments And Real Estate

That They Don't Have A Job, All They Do Is Manage Their Assets"

James L. Painter, To His 14 Year Old Son, Tom

FREE Make More Money With A Small Business

Michael Gerber - The E Myth
Jay Abraham - Money Making Secrets Of A Marketing Genius
Stephen Gibson - Creating Family Prosperity
Brandon Barnum - Making Money With Referrals
Robert Kiyosaki - Make Money With Direct Selling And MLM
Darren Falter - How To Pick A Network Marketing Company

Additional Free Classes SuccessAndMoneyFoundation.Org/Courses

6

Start A Small Business And Give Yourself A Tax Cut

Give yourself a tax cut by starting a small business

How much did you pay in taxes last year?

Would you like to give yourself a tax cut?

What if you could legitimately lower your taxes by 15% to 20% where you can legally deduct everyday items?

There are 2 reasons to start a small business

Cut taxes and to earn extra income

The challenge is that if you are a regular and salaried employee, then you're paying taxes at the highest rates

Small businesses owners

Get to take hundreds of legitimate deductions

You can save thousands of dollars a year by shifting personal expenses to business expenses

Instead of hobbies

Let's create legitimate businesses with the purpose of making money

The real goal is to make more money, Then shift that money to

Step 4. Automatically invest

Another strategy

Is to hire your children

We want you to hire your children so you can teach them how the businesses work and how to make money

This lowers our tax bracket and gets them money to invest

My parents started investment accounts for 70 grand and great grandchildren

That's leaving a legacy

7

3 Ways To Grow Your Business

-Get More Customers

-To Buy More

-To Buy More Often-

8

25

Ways To Make More Money With Your Small Business

A special thanks to Stephen and Bette Gibson

Who are the founders of

Academy for Creating Enterprise

This non-profit has taught tens of thousands of people all over the world how to start and run successful small businesses

For more information on the academy
Go to

The-academy.com

25 Ways To Make More Money With Your Business

1. Start Small; Think Big
2. Sell What People Will Buy
3. Focus, Focus, Focus
4. Use Suggestive Selling
5. Keep Your Personal Money And Business Money Separate
6. Pay Yourself A Livable Salary
7. Keep Good Records
8. Turn Your Inventory Often
9. Don't Eat Your Inventory
10. Continually Look For Improvements
11. Buy Low; Sell High
12. Inspect More, Assume Less
13. Be Nicer Later
14. Work On Your Business 10 Hours A Day
15. Make A Profit Every Day
16. Value Your Customer
17. Hire Slow; Fire Fast
18. Work On Your Business, Not Just In Your Business
19. Buy On Credit; Sell For Cash
20. Use Multiple Suppliers To Get The Best Price
21. Purchase In Bulk
22. Have Written Agreements
23. Increase Sales; Decrease Costs To Earn More Money
24. Daily And Weekly Business Goals
25. Make Your Business Different From Others

9

How To Make Money With The Internet

The internet has changed the world

When I was growing up, there were only a few ways to market

Now, with the use of your phone, you can reach people all over the world

The world is big, but it's small because of technology

Let me show you examples of people who have done well using the internet to deliver their products or services

In our businesses, we have spent millions on marketing, especially on the internet

Let me tell you about Ethan and Jacob, two young guys in their early twenties who decided college wasn't for them

They joined up with me to create a team

I have information and life experience that I want to share

These two young guys went to a specialty course for 14 weeks to learn how to use the internet for programming

The 80/20 principle is crucial,

20% of your activates get you 80% of your results

My friend Kurt Mortensen, a bestselling author who reaches his clients on the internet

He works from home, providing services to clients worldwide

Aaron Allen is a digital nomad, living in foreign countries, providing his services to clients in expensive areas

He can charge a premium price while living inexpensively

To make money on the internet, you must find a good deal,

Only a few fit the criteria

Once you find the right deal, you nail the pricing, the logistics, and then you scale it,

We have multiple free class and books on Amazon and eBay

SuccessAndMoneyFoundation.Org/Courses
SuccessAndMoneyFoundation.org/Downloads

10
Direct Selling
&
Multi-Level Marketing

-Qualify People If They Want to Start a Small Business

-Demonstrate the Compensation Plan

-Enroll 100-200 People

-Help Them Make Money

11
The 5 F's of Real Estate

Find It
Fund It
Fix It
Farm It
Flip It

12
Fix And Flip Properties
Before and After

Only 1%-3% of all the properties that are for sale fit our criteria

Find ways to get the sellers to call you

Until you understand value, everything is worthless

Get a woman on your team, fix up properties for them

Write offers

If you getting more than 1-5 offers accepted, your not getting a good deal

13

Buying Real Estate With Little Or Nothing Down

In my lifetime I've been able to acquire many properties with little or no money down

It all began when I attended
Robert Allen's nothing down seminar

being in college, I really didn't know much about formal real estate investing

And I sat through the two-day seminar, I was overwhelmed with all the options, all the tools that you could use to acquire real estate

And the one thing that I learned more than anything was that it was possible,

Because there was a system, and there were people that were doing it

And so I went to work doing just that

There are 5 things you need to work on

When you are looking at real estate,

You need to find good deals

You need to figure out the funding

Either I'm going to fund it or I'm going to option it

Or

I'm going to bring in a partner to help me

And

Then what's wrong with it

How can I fix this property?

Or

Fix the situation that the seller is in

Are they a don't wanter

Meaning

They don't want the property

and then we're either going to farm it or flip it

Are we going to farm it by renting it out

Or

Flip it for some quick cash

Here are some of our early deals

We were starting out just like many of you

We didn't have any money or credit

This is one of the properties that I'm going to show you that

We owned for 38 years, then we donated it to the foundation

As you know, my wife and I donated $3 million dollars to the success and money foundation

 we did that with our real estate and
Our Berkshire Hathaway stock

So when you think about all these deals, remember, there's the 5 F's

Find it
Fund it
Fix it

Farm it or fix it

The first thing is, don't want you to get too hung up on the pricing

The real key is the percentage of things

Depending on where you live

You can add zeros to the price

And we have students from all over the world that have different currencies

So the price isn't a big deal

Remember, for where you live, you can multiple it by 2, 5 or 10

It's the percentages between things

This little property I found in 1982

 I'm going to use real figures, the value is $80,000

Now, how did I know what the value was?

Because I looked at a lot of properties

I understood what they were worth

And if you want to do well, you need to understand value

Until you understand value

Everything is worthless

The purchase price that I negotiated was $60,000

And again, you could add zeros, you can 10 times this 5 times this

It doesn't matter

The difference was that I was buying it for 20% below market

I thought that the property was worth $80,000

This gentleman had bought it years before

And he bought it for $30,000, and again,

I don't care if it's $3 million or $300,000, whatever it is

It's the strategy I want you to understand

But he had bought it for a much lower price

And so I was able to buy that property off of him at a bargain price

We agreed on the price, and I said we can do 1 or 2 things

I can go to the bank, and I can get you all your money

And you can cash out and get your money

Or

I can do what we call seller finance

Historically

When people were selling farms to each other, the bank wouldn't loan them any money

So

They would do owner financing

And

Make payments to the seller

We agreed on the price of $60,000

With a $5,000 down payment

That means I still owe him $55,000

I asked him why he

Why was he selling

And

What was he going to do with the money?

He said that he had bought it 15 years earlier for $30,000

He lived next door and he also managed it

Which he didn't like

He was tired of the management

What he wanted was the monthly payment

Plus,

He didn't want to pay a bunch of money in taxes

So I made him a deal to buy it for

$60,000 with $5,000 down

Then make monthly payments

Of

$591.03 a month

For 15 years at 10%

4 units were rented at $200 each

So,

We were bringing in $800 a month in rent

Again, just add zero's

It's the percentages that count

Every month I would collect the rent and send him a check

Why did he agree to this deal?

Because

All he wanted was the monthly payments

Plus,

He didn't want to pay a bunch of money in taxes

Over the years, with interest

I paid him over $100,000

Which I got from the renters

We kept that property for 38 years and eventually donated it to the foundation

The purchase price when we bought it was $60,000

When we donated it

The price was $490,000

My small down payment of less than $5,000

Had turned into $490,000 plus all the positive cash flow

Basically, 100x my initial investment

14

Nothing Down
Just Add Zero's

This is the same technique

 I just added a bunch of zero's

I used this technique many times

I found an owner that had 7 four unit buildings

For a total of 28 units

They were mismanaged

I bought them with nothing down

And

Made payments to the seller

Just like the earlier example

A year later

He asked if I would pay him off because he had another deal he wanted to invest in

I asked for a large discount

And

Got it

Since I owned them,

I went to the mortgage company and refinanced them to pay off existing debt

Our purchase price was $250,000 x 7 = $1,750,000

We owned them for 27 years

And sold them for

$500,000 x 7 = $3,500,000

Over the 27 years we owned them

Tenants paid us rent and we paid the mortgage

When we sold them to invest in other properties

They were all free and clear

Netting us $3,500,000 on nothing down

We used that technique multiple time

Eventually we bought 20

Four unit buildings

Over time they increased in value to $500,000 each

We later sold them to invest in other real estate projects

20 buildings x $500,000 = $10,000,000 profit

When we started the foundation

We donated 3 of the four unit buildings and 2 houses

Plus

Some Warren Buffett stock

A total of

$3,000,000 to fund the foundation

Were now giving that money away to help students all over the world

15

50

Nothing Down Techniques

Robert Allen is the author of the book

Nothing Down
"How to buy real estate with little or nothing down"

I highly recommend you read his book

Robert is also a friend and supporter of the foundation

The foundation would not exist if it wasn't for him

Here are his 50 nothing down techniques

1. The Seller
2. The Buyer
3. The Realtor
4. The Renters
5. The Property
6. Hard-Money Lenders
7. Underlying Mortgages
8. Investors
9. Partners
10. Options
11. Assume Sellers Obligations
12. Using Talents, Not Money
13. Borrow Against Life Insurance Policy
14. Anything Goes
15. Creation Of Paper
16. The Two-Way Exchange
17. The Three-Way Exchange
18. Lemonading
19. Borrowing The Realtors Commission
20. Rents
21. Deposits
22. Splitting Off Furniture And Other Items
23. Splitting Off Part Of The Property
24. Small Amounts Of Money From Different Banks
25. Cash By Mail Companies
26. Credit Cards
27. Home Improvement Loans
28. Home Equity Loans

29. Refinance Boat, Car, Stereo Or Personal Property
30. VA Loans
31. FHA Loans
32. The Second Mortgage Crank
33. Variation Of The Crank: Seller Refinance
34. Buy Low, Refinance High
35. Using Discounts From Holders Of Mortgages
36. Moving The Mortgage
37. Creative Refinance Of Underlying Mortgages
38. Pulling Cash Out Of Buildings You Own But Don't Want To Sell
39. Making A Partner Of The Holder Of An Underlying Mortgage
40. Selling Of Second Trust Notes
41. Borrow Partners Financial Statement
42. Borrow Partners Money For Down Payment
43. Borrow Partners Money For Down Payment Until Your Money Comes
44. You're Cashflow/My Equity Or Some Combination
45. You Put Up The Cash; I Put Up The Time And Expertise
46. The Rolling Option
47. Equity For Options
48. Sale Option Back
49. Earnest Money Option
50. Lease With An Option To Purchase

Free Course You Can Take On Real Estate

Robert Allen - The Road To Wealth
Robert Allen - The Real Estate Launch

SuccessAndMoneyFoundation.Org/Courses

Free Books You Can Download On Real Estate

Mark Haroldsen - Wake Up The Financial Genius Inside You

SuccessAndMoneyFoundation.Org /Books

Free Downloads On Real Estate

Real Estate Bargain Finder
Property Scoring System
Find It, Fund It, Farm It
Nothing Down Real Estate Techniques
Zero To $1,000,000 On $49 A Month

SuccessAndMoneyFoundation.Org /Downloads

16

Making Money With Real Estate

There are many ways that you can make an additional chunk of money with real estate

The great thing about real estate is that it keeps up with inflation

It brings in income

I want to thank Robert Allen for allowing us to use some of his wonderful material in the foundation

This is our legacy project, I suggest you start with 2 books

Mark Haroldsen "How to Wake up the Financial Genius Inside You"

And Robert Allen books, The Road to Wealth, Multiple Streams of Income

For free books and downloads go to
Successandmoneyfoundation.org /books
Successandmoneyfoundation.org/downloads

Here are some of the nothing down techniques I've used

The first one is seller financing; this is where you make payments to the seller

Number 10

Supply the seller with what he needs

A seller is selling a property for some reason

Why are they selling it?

What are they going to do with the money, and what do they need?

I've done many properties where the seller just wanted the monthly payments

He didn't want to be the manager

He didn't want to have to fix up the properties

And so we did a combination of those earlier techniques, and we got him what he wanted, which was monthly payments or taking over the seller's obligation

Many times people have a loan on the property

They want to walk away and be done with it

And then we take over those payments

We take them subject to the existing obligations that are on that property

Number 12 is using talents, not money

Do you have something they need, you can exchange for

I did one property where I sold it, and I needed some help with some plumbing and some help fixing up properties

The guys that bought it off of me didn't have enough money for the down payment that we needed, so he traded for work

They used their talents as builders to finish up some jobs

Number 20 is rent

I've done this one with the rents and the security deposits

One of the first properties I did was a 4-unit building, and we were able to close on the first of the month

So we got all the security deposits and that became mine because when they move out, I have to pay the deposit back

So that was credited to me, plus all the rents were due on the first, and so I got credit for those

That reduced my down payment

Number 22

Splitting off the furniture or other items

I've done this multiple times where I was able to split off the furniture or washer and dryers

I'd sell them to recoup my cash

I even did one where there was a speedboat and a mobile home

Number 27

Home improvement loans and line of credit

A good way to be able to borrow enough money is a home improvement loan

And that's a good way to be able to get into that property without as much money down, because you can go borrow against that property on the loan

Number 34

Buy low, refinance high
This is one where we bought properties for a certain price, and then we were able to refinance it at a higher amount

And get back all the capital we put in

Number 35

Is to use discounts from mortgage holders

I've done this multiple times where there was a mortgage on the property and we got a discount in order to pay them off in cash

On one set of buildings, we did

We've got three hundred thousand dollars in discounts because they wanted their cash

and he decided that he didn't want to take those payments for the next 20 years

So we asked for a big discount and they gave it to us, then we just simply refinanced it and were able to pay him out

Number 40

Selling a second trustee note, you can create a note where you owe somebody some money that's tied to that property

And then you can sell it to somebody else that wants to collect it, and they will pay cash for that
Number 42

Borrow partner's money for down payment

This is interesting

And I've seen this in all kinds of areas in deals where there are getting millions of dollars from investors

The investors are coming up with the monies for the big down payments, and then the general partners are getting loans on property

You put up the cash, I put up the expertise

Number 47

Options

This is a big one that we did many, many times where we got the right to lease a property and an option to buy it

So we would make monthly payments on that property as a lease, and we had the right to buy it for a certain price in the future

And then we would fix it up and turn around and resell it to someone else
We would exercise our option and buy it for one price and sell it for the other price

That happens all day long

Everywhere you go

Walmart, for example

They don't own the products

They just sell them

Amazon is the same way

Other people own that product
And amazon sells that product on consignment

And so there's many different ways that you can buy property with
little or none of your own money

"Don't Wait To Buy Real Estate, Buy Real Estate And Wait"

Robert Allen

17

Is Debt Good
Or
Bad

Is debt good or bad?

Well, it really depends on what you do with the debt

Good debt is when you can borrow money to buy things that go up in value, that produce income

If it doesn't produce income and it doesn't go up in value, you should not be borrowing money

Debt

It's a double-edged sword

If you can use debt to buy long-term real estate that has a positive cash flow

The renters make payments and pay off the debt

That's good debt

If you borrow money on a credit card you have to make the payments

That's bad debt

The rule of 72 says that if you borrow money at 21%

It takes 3-4 years for that debt to double in cost

Mathematically,

It's very hard to get out of that kind of debt

Is it wise to get into debt to go to college?

It all depends if what you learn will make you more money in the future

If you go to school and major in humanities or music

Will you make you money?

And if it doesn't, then you shouldn't do it

My 2 techno-wizards that work with me

They went to 16 weeks of online school to learn how to program

They make a lot of money programming

And I'm happy to pay for it because I'm able to take my products and services and get the information out about the foundation

They went to a very short school to learn a specific skill

The better their skill, the more money that they can charge

 Debt can be good, and debt can be bad

Your goal is to figure out how to get a rate of return

On the debt

When you borrow money, you should ask yourself

Can I get a rate of return on this?

Is this going to make me more money in the future?

And if it's not making you more money, then don't do it

18

Step Two
Separate Your Money

Manage Your Money
On
1 Piece Of Paper

Step number 1 is to make more money

Step number 2 is to separate your money into 3 groups

The biggest problem with money management or cash flow management is that people run out of money before they run out of month

The solution to cash flow management is to run out a month before you run out of money

The system must be so simple that you can manage it on one piece of paper

I want to introduce you to the cash flow tracker

This cash flow tracker is free

You can go to

<u>Successandmoneyfoundation.org/downloads</u>

There are all kinds of online apps that you can use as well

Dave Ramsey has a really good one called every dollar

The cash flow tracker helps you pace
Your spending through the month

That's the key to the cash flow tracker

After the month is over, you can put your expenses into QuickBooks
or a spreadsheet,

The real key is that we want to be able to pace ourselves

There are 5 steps to financial freedom

Number 1 is to make more money

Number 2 is to separate it into 3 groups

Number 3 is to give to individuals, church and charity

Number 4 is to automatically invest,

Number 5 is to save and spend

The tracker takes these first 5 areas and puts them on one piece of paper

The tracker takes these first 5 areas

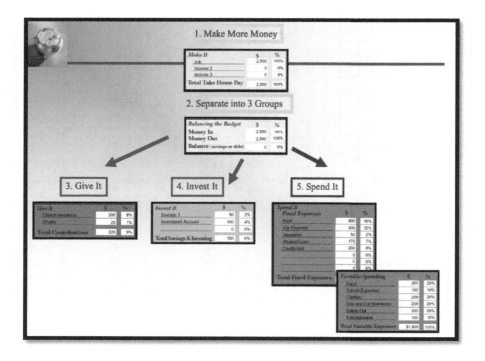

And puts them on one piece of paper

Month _____

Money Made Easy
Spending Tracker

Make It

	$	%
DAD's take home	3,000	50%
Mom's take home	2,000	33%
Other income	1,000	17%
Take Home Pay	6,000	100%

Give It

	$	%
Charity - Unitus Fund	500	8%

Invest It

	$	%
Savings - Wells Fargo	250	4%
401K MUTUAL FUND	250	4%

Spend It
Fixed Expenses

	$	%
Home Mortgage	1,500	25%
Auto Loan	300	5%
Insurance	100	2%
Student Loan	200	3%
Chase Visa Card	400	7%
Second Mortgage	500	8%
Property Taxes	300	5%
Food & Dining	700	12%
Total Fixed Expenses	$4,000	67%

Variable Spending

	$	%
Dad's spending	100	2%
Mom's spending	200	3%
Kids allowance	100	2%
Family recreation	300	5%
Gas & Auto exp	500	8%
Clothing	150	3%
Total Variable Expenses	$1,350	23%

Balancing the Budget

	$	%
Money In	6,000	100%
Money Out	6,350	106%
Balance (savings or debt)	-350	

MONEY MADE EASY

www.moneymadeeasy.com

Day	Dad's spending $ 100	Mom's spending $ 200	Kids allowance $ 100	Family recreation $ 300	Gas & Auto exp $ 500	Clothing $ 150
1	97	194	97	291	486	146
2	94	189	94	283	471	141
3	91	183	91	274	457	137
4	89	177	89	266	443	133
5	86	171	86	257	429	129
6	83	166	83	249	414	124
7	80	160	80	240	400	120
8	77	154	77	231	386	116
9	74	149	74	223	371	111
10	71	143	71	214	357	107
11	69	137	69	206	343	103
12	66	131	66	197	329	99
13	63	126	63	189	314	94
14	60	120	60	180	300	90
15	57	114	57	171	286	86
16	54	109	54	163	271	81
17	51	103	51	154	257	77
18	49	97	49	146	243	73
19	46	91	46	137	229	69
20	43	86	43	129	214	64
21	40	80	40	120	200	60
22	37	74	37	111	186	56
23	34	69	34	103	171	51
24	31	63	31	94	157	47
25	29	57	29	86	143	43
26	26	51	26	77	129	39
27	23	46	23	69	114	34
28	20	40	20	60	100	30
29	17	34	17	51	86	26
30	14	29	14	43	71	21
31	11	23	11	34	57	17
	9	17	9	26	43	13
	6	11	6	17	29	9
	3	6	3	9	14	4
	0	0	0	0	0	0
Over						

As you're filling out this form is

Number 1. Make more money

1. Make More Money

Make It	$	%
Job	2,500	100%
Income 2	0	0%
Income 3	0	0%
Total Take Home Pay	2,500	100%

This is where you're going to add your take-home pay from your job, your wife's job, or other income that's coming in

Number 2 is to separate it

2. Separate into 3 Groups

Balancing the Budget	$	%
Money In	2,500	100%
Money Out	2,500	100%
Balance (savings or debt)	0	0%

This is where we see money coming in and money going out

This is not so much a hardcore budget as it is a cash flow tracker

You want to see how much money you've got coming in, and then you need to allocate where the money is going out

You're going to allocate it into 3 areas

Number 3 is to give to individuals, churches and charities

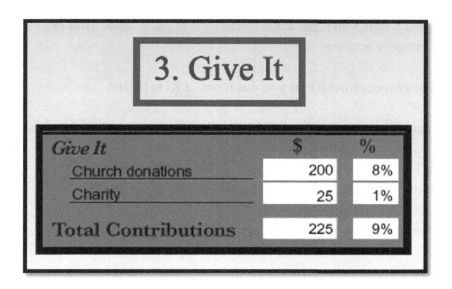

3. Give It

Give It	$	%
Church donations	200	8%
Charity	25	1%
Total Contributions	225	9%

Number 4 is to automatically invest,

4. Invest It

Invest It	$	%
Savings 1	50	2%
Investment Account	100	4%
	0	0%
Total Savings & Investing	150	6%

This is where you'll put it into your ROTH IRA, 401k, IRA or investment account

I highly recommend that you put it into a ROTH IRA

when you put it into a ROTH IRA, you don't get a tax break today

But all the money you put in and all the growth, which could be multiples of that,

You never, ever have to pay any taxes on it,

Any of it

Number 5 is to spend

Now, there are 2 kinds of spending: fixed expenses and variable expenses

Fixed expenses are things on a monthly basis like rent, car payment, insurance, student loans, or credit cards

Variable expenses are things like food, school expenses, clothing, auto, eating out, or entertainment

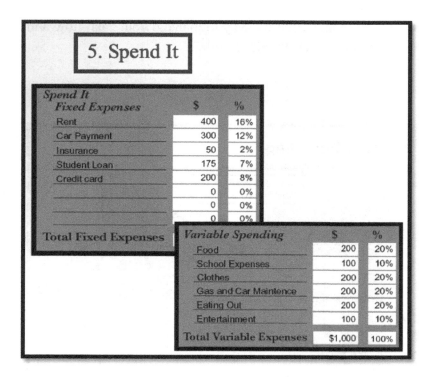

5. Spend It

Spend It

Fixed Expenses	$	%
Rent	400	16%
Car Payment	300	12%
Insurance	50	2%
Student Loan	175	7%
Credit card	200	8%
	0	0%
	0	0%
	0	0%
Total Fixed Expenses		

Variable Spending	$	%
Food	200	20%
School Expenses	100	10%
Clothes	200	20%
Gas and Car Maintence	200	20%
Eating Out	200	20%
Entertainment	100	10%
Total Variable Expenses	$1,000	100%

As you fill out the variable expenses

It will fill in the cash flow thermometers

It helps you keep track of your variable expenses through the month

It provides a visual representation of your spending, and you can adjust your spending as needed to ensure you don't run out of money before the month ends

This is a simple and effective way to manage your cash flow and work towards financial freedom

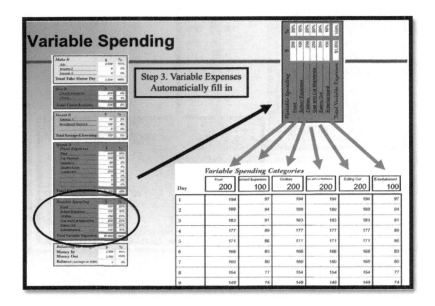

As you spend the variable money

You simply subtract that amount from your column

Variable Spending Categories

Day	Food 200	School Expenses 100	Clothes 200	Gas and
1	194	97	194	
	189	94	189	
3	183	91	183	
4	177	89	177	
5	171	86	171	
6	166	83	166	
7	$160 160	80	160	
8	154	77	154	
	149	74	149	

In this example, if you spend $40 from your food budget, you simply subtract the $40 from the $200 budget

You now have $160 left

On the left side column, if it is the 4th of the month

You are spending your food budget faster than the month

If it's the 8th of the month, you're right on pace

The ideas is to run out of month, before you run out of money

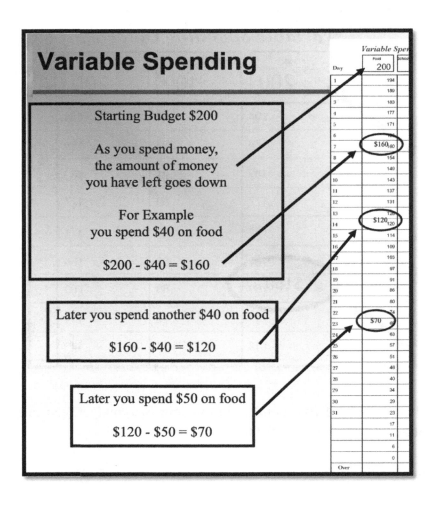

We have also added 4 additional days to help you pace your spending, so you'll have extra money at the end of the month

With that extra money, put it into your investment account

19

Cash Flow Statement

A Cash Flow statement simply tracks the FLOW of your money,

Do you have more money coming in than going out

All money coming in

Minus

All money going out

Equals Net Cash Flow

(+) Income

(-) Charity, Investments And Expenses

(=) Net Cash Flow

20
Income Statement

An Income Statement simply tells you if you are profitable or not

All Income coming in

Minus

All Charity and Expenses going out

Equals Net Income

(+) Income

(-) Charity & Expenses

(=) Net Income

21
Net Worth Statement

A Net worth Statement simply tells you how much your worth

All asset and anything of value

Minus

All loans

Equals Net Worth

(+) Assets

(Anything Of Value)

(-) Loans

(=) Net Worth

22

Give To Individuals,

Churches

&

Charities

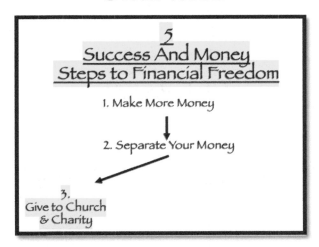

Giving is a spiritual law and a business law

Zig Ziglar said

"The only way you can get what you want out of life is to help other people get what they want out of life"

Robert Allen
Taught me about giving money at a very, very young age

Mark Victor Hansen,
Author of "Chicken Soup for the Soul"

Gives money to different charities for each of the books that are sold

Paul Newman

Has donated over $500 million dollars

From the profits of Newman's own food products

Warren Buffett

He's giving away 99% of his net worth to charity
Bill gates

Bill gates not only gave the money, but he also was giving his time
and his energy to solve a lot of the problems around the world

"The Secret To Living Is Giving"
Tony Robbins

"Make A Difference, Make It Happen, Every Life Is Precious"
Thomas Painter

23

Automatically Invest

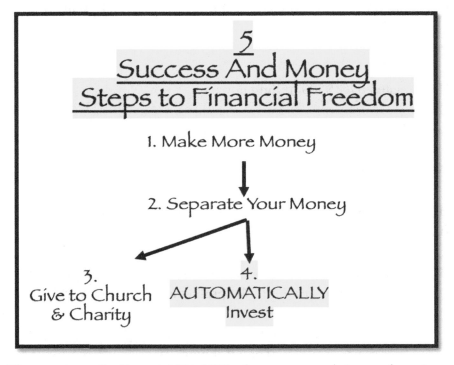

If you automatically put 10%-15% of your money into you long term investment account

Invest it in the Berkshire Hathaway or the S&P 500 (500 largest US companies) and let it grow

It will solve the vast majority of your financial problems when you get older

24

Does Money Grow On Trees?

Does money grow on trees?

Would you like to grow your own money tree?

What kind of seed would you use to grow a money tree?

You'd need a penny

If you didn't water your money tree, would it grow?

You need to water your tree with dollars

Watch your money tree grow

You're going to plant a penny, and then it's going to grow and grow and grow and grow and grow and grow and grow

It's going to take years for it to grow, and then eventually, it will produce fruit

That tree will produce more fruit every year, just like a cherry tree, apple tree, or a peach tree produces fruit that you can trade for cash

A money tree does the same thing,

Very successful people have a lot of money trees

Would you like to have a tree that grows a million dollars?

This is what it would look like

Well, it doesn't quite look like that,

But this is kind of a fun way to look at it

You need to water your tree

How many dollars do you water your tree with?

It all depends on your age

So how old are you?

You can see this is a picture that was taken many years ago of some of my nieces and nephews and some of my own kids

This is how much money they need to invest on a monthly basis to have $1,000,000 when they turn 65

So you'll notice down at the very end, is Jackson

He only needs $16 a month all the way up to Carlee, who is age 19 and needs $86 a month

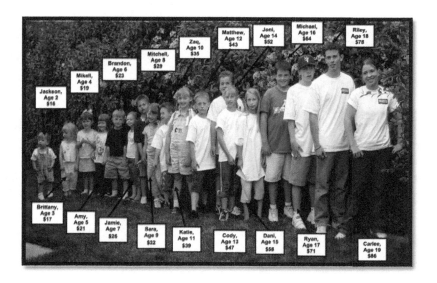

Why?

Because they have a longer timeframe

So if you find your age on this chart,

This is how many dollars you need to put away on a monthly basis starting at this age until age 65 to have a million dollars

now, that assumes that you get a 10% rate of return

you can see a 10-year-old in the first column only needs $35 a month,

Whereas a 19-year-old would need $86 a month

Many people and kids don't have that kind of money

And so what we want you to do is ask your parents if they'll match part of it so you only need half as much money

Age	Monthly	Age	Monthly	Age	Monthly	Age	Monthly	Age	Monthly
1	$14	16	$64	31	$292	46	$1,479	61	$17,029
2	$16	17	$71	32	$324	47	$1,665	62	$23,934
3	$17	18	$78	33	$359	48	$1,879	63	$37,812
4	$19	19	$86	34	$398	49	$2,126	64	$79,583
5	$21	20	$95	35	$442	50	$2,413		
6	$23	21	$106	36	$491	51	$2,749		
7	$26	22	$117	37	$546	52	$3,145	Monthly	
8	$29	23	$129	38	$608	53	$3,617	savings	
9	$32	24	$143	39	$676	54	$4,187	required	
10	$35	25	$158	40	$754	55	$4,882	to reach	
11	$39	26	$175	41	$841	56	$5,745	$1 Million	
12	$43	27	$194	42	$938	57	$6,841	by	
13	$47	28	$215	43	$1,049	58	$8,268	age 65	
14	$52	29	$238	44	$1,174	59	$10,193	(10% rate)	
15	$58	30	$263	45	$1,317	60	$12,914		

You can see that if someone started at age one in the top left-hand corner,

They only need $14 a month,

And over time by age 65, that would turn into a million dollars

That's at a 10% rate of return with long-term stock

Berkshire Hathaway, the S&P 500 has been averaging between 8% and 12% over the years

Some years it goes up, some years it goes down,
But over a long period of time, that's about what it's done

You'll notice in the second column, at the very top, an age 16-year-old only needs $64

But look how it changes for a 31-year-old it's $292,

A 64-year-old is $1,400,

And a 61-year-old is $17,000

This is all about compounding and having time for your investments to grow

That's why it's so important that you start at an early age

The one thing that every adult agrees with me on is that they wish they would have started earlier

They wish they would have started investing and putting money away and having that money work for them

So these are the steps to growing your own money tree

25
Wealth Formula

The Wealth Formula is a how you create wealth, you simply add monthly investments to your investment account, have those investments go up in value and do it for a long period of time, that will create wealth

Monthly Investment
(X)
Increase In Value
(X)
Length Of Time
(=)
Wealth

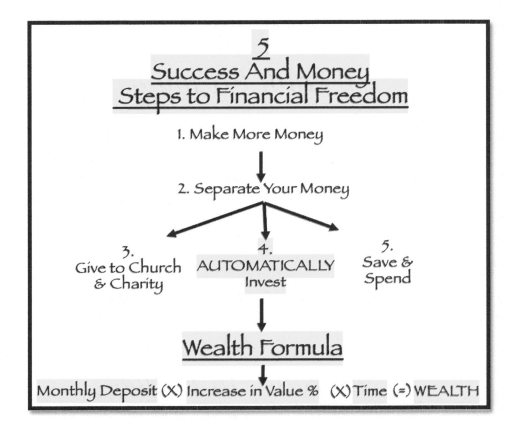

5
Success And Money
Steps to Financial Freedom

1. Make More Money

2. Separate Your Money

3.
Give to Church
& Charity

4.
AUTOMATICALLY
Invest

5.
Save &
Spend

Wealth Formula

Monthly Deposit (X) Increase in Value % (X) Time (=) WEALTH

26

How Long Does It Take for An Asset or Loan To Double In Value or Cost?

Introducing the rule of 72,

It is a simple equation to find out how many years it will take to for

your money to double in value or cost

The formula is based on your interest rate

The equation is

$$72 / 6 = 12$$

72 (Divided By) Interest Rate (=) Length Of Time To Double

It takes 12 years

Another way to solve it is

$$6 (X) 12 (=) 72$$

Interest Rate (X) Time (=) 72

27

How Long Does It Take For Your Credit Card To Double In Cost At 21% Interest Rate

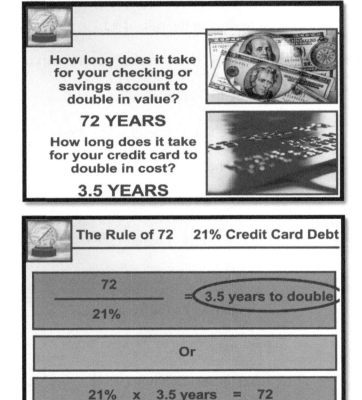

28

How Much Would You Have ?

If You Put A Dollar A Day In The Bank

For 66 Years And Receive 0% Interest?

What a difference a dollar a day will make in your life!

How much would you have if you put a dollar a day in a piggy bank and you did that from the day you were born until you turned 66 years of age?

How much would you have?

The Correct Answer Is $24,090

Rate	How much in 66 years?
0%	$ 24,090

29

How Much Would You?

If You Put A Dollar A Day In The Bank

For 66 Years And Receive 3% Interest?

But if you took that same dollar a day in your savings account, and the bank paid you 3% a year for the same 66 years,

You're getting a 3% rate of return

So for every $100 you put in there, you'll make $3 worth of interest,

And then the next year you'll have $103

The Correct Answer On This One Is $75,736

So A Dollar A Day With A 3% Rate Of Return Turns Into $75,736

Rate	How much in 66 years?
0%	$ 24,090
3%	$ 75,736

30

How Much Would You Have?

If You Put A Dollar A Day In The Stock Market

With 10% Appreciation

How much would you have if you put a dollar a day in the stock market and got a 10% rate of return for 66 years?

Some years it goes up, some years it goes down, but over a long period of time, we're looking for about a 10% rate of return

Here's an example of the stock market:

McDonald's is owned by thousands of people

You can buy a small portion of McDonald's by buying its stock

How much would you have if you went to McDonald's instead of buying a drink you bought a small part of the company?

A Dollar A Day With A 10% Increase In Value For 66 Years Turns
Into
$2.6 Million Dollars

Rate	How much in 66 years?
0%	$ 24,090
3%	$ 75,736
10%	$ 2,607,064

31

How Much Would You Owe

If You Spent A Dollar A Day On A Credit Card

21% Interest Rate

Now, how much would you owe if you charged a dollar a day on your credit card,

And the credit card company is charging you 21% interest for 66 years?

Now, instead of investing in McDonald's,

You go to McDonald's and buy a drink using your credit card

You don't pay off the balance each month, the credit card company charges you 21% interest

How much would you owe if you charged a dollar a day on your credit card at 21% interest?

The Correct Answer Is $1.6 Billion Dollars

Rate	How much in 66 years?
0%	$ 24,090
3%	$ 75,736
10%	$ 2,607,064
21%	$1,611,877,660

32
Which Would You Rather Have?

$1,000 A Day Each Day for 40 Days

Or

A Penny A Doubled Each Day for 40 Days?

Which would you rather have?

1 penny doubled every day for 40 days

$1,000 each day for 40 days

Q: What can you buy for a $1,000?
A: A computer or a stereo.

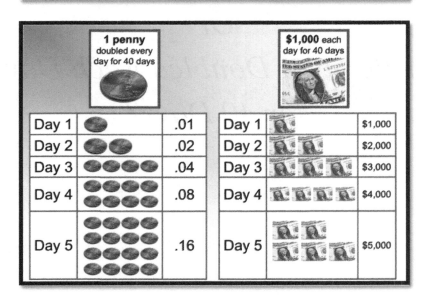

	1 penny doubled every day for 40 days			$1,000 each day for 40 days	
Day 1		.01	Day 1		$1,000
Day 2		.02	Day 2		$2,000
Day 3		.04	Day 3		$3,000
Day 4		.08	Day 4		$4,000
Day 5		.16	Day 5		$5,000

Penny Wins

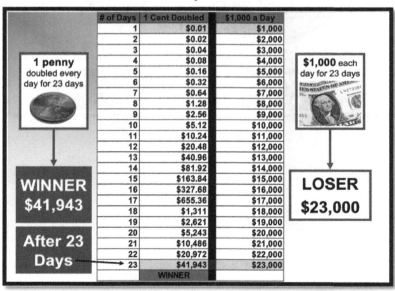

# of Days	1 Cent Doubled	$1,000 a Day
1	$0.01	$1,000
2	$0.02	$2,000
3	$0.04	$3,000
4	$0.08	$4,000
5	$0.16	$5,000
6	$0.32	$6,000
7	$0.64	$7,000
8	$1.28	$8,000
9	$2.56	$9,000
10	$5.12	$10,000
11	$10.24	$11,000
12	$20.48	$12,000
13	$40.96	$13,000
14	$81.92	$14,000
15	$163.84	$15,000
16	$327.68	$16,000
17	$655.36	$17,000
18	$1,311	$18,000
19	$2,621	$19,000
20	$5,243	$20,000
21	$10,486	$21,000
22	$20,972	$22,000
23	$41,943	$23,000
	WINNER	

1 penny doubled every day for 23 days

WINNER $41,943

After 23 Days

$1,000 each day for 23 days

LOSER $23,000

Which Would You Rather Have?

A Penny A Day Doubled Each Day for 40 Days
Or
$10,000 Each Day For 40 Days

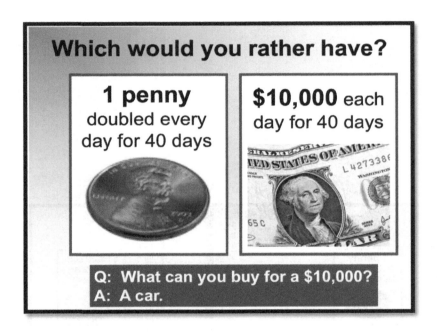

Penny Wins

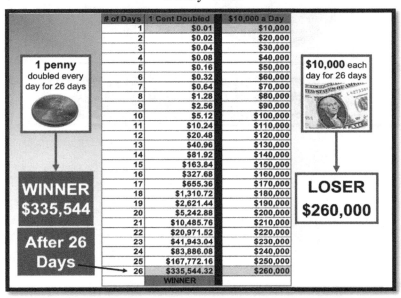

# of Days	1 Cent Doubled	$10,000 a Day
1	$0.01	$10,000
2	$0.02	$20,000
3	$0.04	$30,000
4	$0.08	$40,000
5	$0.16	$50,000
6	$0.32	$60,000
7	$0.64	$70,000
8	$1.28	$80,000
9	$2.56	$90,000
10	$5.12	$100,000
11	$10.24	$110,000
12	$20.48	$120,000
13	$40.96	$130,000
14	$81.92	$140,000
15	$163.84	$150,000
16	$327.68	$160,000
17	$655.36	$170,000
18	$1,310.72	$180,000
19	$2,621.44	$190,000
20	$5,242.88	$200,000
21	$10,485.76	$210,000
22	$20,971.52	$220,000
23	$41,943.04	$230,000
24	$83,886.08	$240,000
25	$167,772.16	$250,000
26	$335,544.32	$260,000
	WINNER	

1 penny doubled every day for 26 days

WINNER $335,544

After 26 Days

$10,000 each day for 26 days

LOSER $260,000

Which Would You Rather Have?

A Penny A Day Doubled
Or
$100,000 Each Day For 40 Days

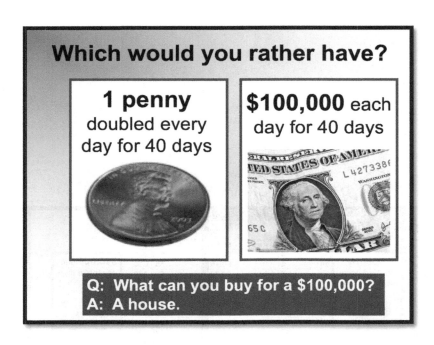

Penny Wins

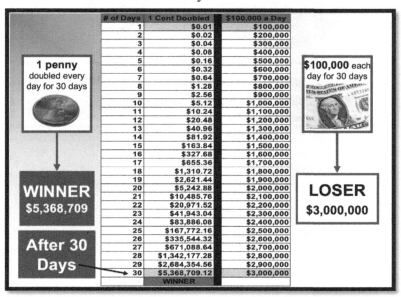

1 penny doubled every day for 30 days

WINNER $5,368,709

After 30 Days

$100,000 each day for 30 days

LOSER $3,000,000

# of Days	1 Cent Doubled	$100,000 a Day
1	$0.01	$100,000
2	$0.02	$200,000
3	$0.04	$300,000
4	$0.08	$400,000
5	$0.16	$500,000
6	$0.32	$600,000
7	$0.64	$700,000
8	$1.28	$800,000
9	$2.56	$900,000
10	$5.12	$1,000,000
11	$10.24	$1,100,000
12	$20.48	$1,200,000
13	$40.96	$1,300,000
14	$81.92	$1,400,000
15	$163.84	$1,500,000
16	$327.68	$1,600,000
17	$655.36	$1,700,000
18	$1,310.72	$1,800,000
19	$2,621.44	$1,900,000
20	$5,242.88	$2,000,000
21	$10,485.76	$2,100,000
22	$20,971.52	$2,200,000
23	$41,943.04	$2,300,000
24	$83,886.08	$2,400,000
25	$167,772.16	$2,500,000
26	$335,544.32	$2,600,000
27	$671,088.64	$2,700,000
28	$1,342,177.28	$2,800,000
29	$2,684,354.56	$2,900,000
30	$5,368,709.12	$3,000,000
	WINNER	

Which Would You Rather Have?

A Penny A Day Doubled
Or
$1,000,000 Each Day For 40 Days

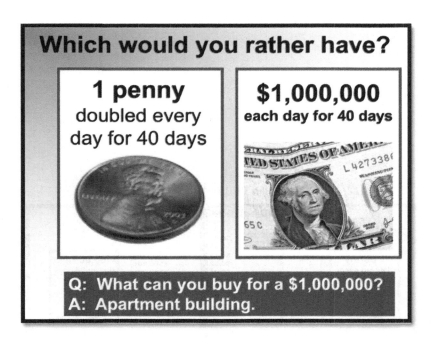

Penny Wins

1 penny doubled every day for 40 days			$1,000,000 each day for 40 days
	5	$0.16	$5,000,000
	6	$0.32	$6,000,000
	7	$0.64	$7,000,000
	8	$1.28	$8,000,000
	9	$2.56	$9,000,000
	10	$5.12	$10,000,000
	11	$10.24	$11,000,000
	12	$20.48	$12,000,000
	13	$40.96	$13,000,000
	14	$81.92	$14,000,000
	15	$163.84	$15,000,000
	16	$327.68	$16,000,000
	17	$655.36	$17,000,000
	18	$1,310.72	$18,000,000
	19	$2,621.44	$19,000,000
	20	$5,242.88	$20,000,000
	21	$10,485.76	$21,000,000
	22	$20,971.52	$22,000,000
	23	$41,943.04	$23,000,000
	24	$83,886.08	$24,000,000
	25	$167,772.16	$25,000,000
	26	$335,544.32	$26,000,000
	27	$671,088.64	$27,000,000
WINNER $5,497,558,139	28	$1,342,177.28	$28,000,000
	29	$2,684,354.56	$29,000,000
	30	$5,368,709.12	$30,000,000
	31	$10,737,418.24	$31,000,000
	32	$21,474,836.48	$32,000,000
	33	$42,949,672.96	$33,000,000
	34	$85,899,345.92	$34,000,000
That's more than $5 Billion!	35	$171,798,691.84	$35,000,000
	36	$343,597,383.68	$36,000,000
	37	$687,194,767.36	$37,000,000
	38	$1,374,389,534.72	$38,000,000
	39	$2,748,779,069.44	$39,000,000
	40	$5,497,558,138.88	$40,000,000
		WINNER	LOSER $40,000,000

You Would Need

$137,438,953

A Day For 40 Days

To Equal

A Penny Doubled

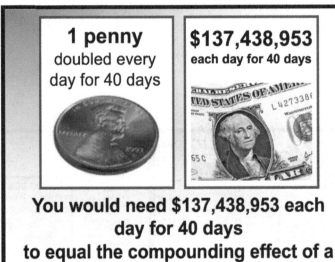

33

*What Items Go Down
In Value?*

Cars

Electronics

Computers

34

What Items Go Up In Value?

Stocks

Real Estate

Business

35
What Kind Of Accounts Could You Use?

Bank Account
Saving Account
Investment Account
Retirement Account

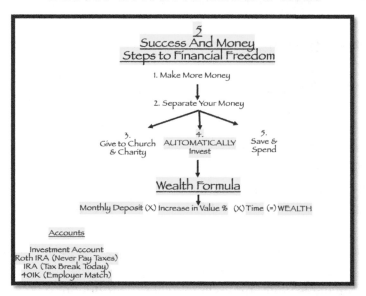

Investment Account

Open an investment account and automatically invest each month

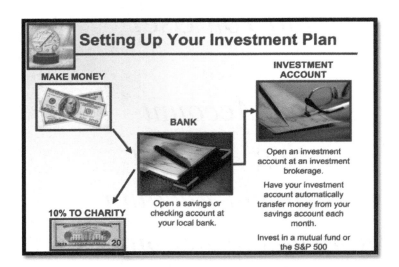

Retirement Accounts

Put as much money as you can in these accounts in this order

#1. 401k
Some employers offer a 401k retirement account for their employees

Each month as employee, you can have 3%-6% of YOUR salary automatically invested in the 401k retirement account

Most match between 3%-6% of what the employee puts into their account
The advantage is your employer matches, your doubling your money

Strategy: Put in as much as your employer will match

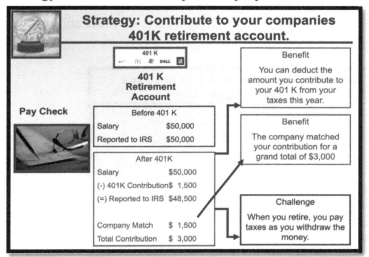

#2. Roth IRA

You can put up to $6,000 a year into your Roth IRA, The advantage is you don't pay any taxes on any of the money when you retire

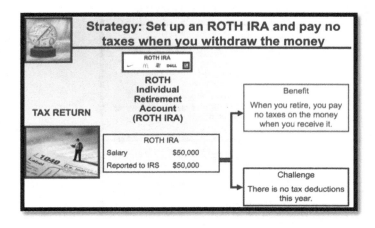

#3. IRA (Individual Retirement Account)

After you have maxed on putting money into your 401K and Roth IRA, Put money into your IRA

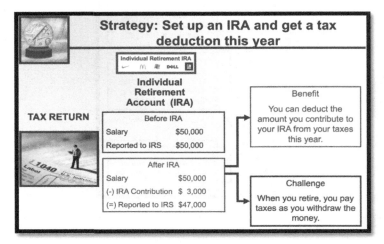

The next chart show how much you would have if you did $300 a month in each of the different options

Investment Account Options

	Monthly	Company Contribution	Tax Deduction this year	# of years	% Increase in value	Value	Taxes at Retirement (30%)	Net at Retirement
Investment Account	$300	No	No	40	10%	$144,000 Monthly contribution $1,608,666 appreciation	$-482,600	$1,126,066
IRA	$300	No	Yes	40	10%	$1,752,666	-$525,799	$1,226,866
Roth IRA	$300	No	No	40	10%	$1,752,666	-$0	$1,752,666
401K	$300	Yes $300	Yes	40	10%	$3,505,333	-$1,051,600	$2,453,733

Which program is best for you?
Would you rather pay taxes on the
Seed (Investment Account, Roth IRA) or on the
Harvest (IRA, 401K)

36

Loan Vs Own

Loan: Checking, Savings CD's, Bonds and Loans

Own: Stock and Real Estate

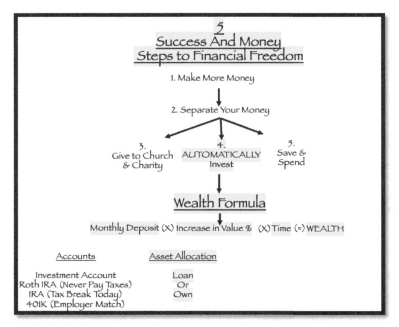

37

4 Ways To Invest In The Stock Market

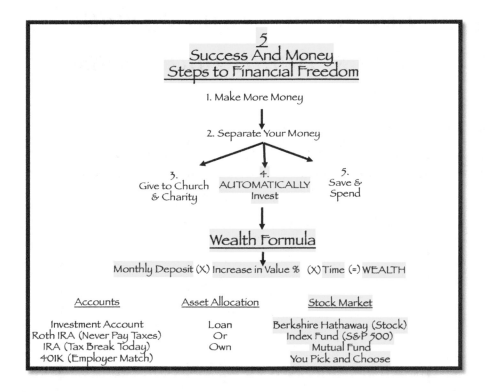

There are 4 ways to invest in the stock market

You can pick and choose

Invest in a mutual fund

Invest in an index fund

Or my favorite is Berkshire Hathaway

What does each of these mean?

Picking and choosing

Is when you pick and choose which stocks you want to buy or sell

Mutual fund

Is when you hire a profession manager to pick and choose the stocks

Index fund

Is when an investment company invests in a group of stock

Like

The S&P 500

Which is the 500 largest companies in America

That do business worldwide

Or

Dow 30

This is a group of 30 companies

1 from each industry

For example

There is a computer, software, automobile, food company etc.

Or

Or you can do the last one which I like is Berkshire Hathaway, BRK.b

Berkshire Hathaway is a company that Warren Buffett controls

Its roots are in insurance, business and investments

The difference is that it is a stock

The reason we like this so much is that there are thousands of stocks and companies

You can pick and choose which companies you want to buy and invest in

The problem is most people spend all their time and energy trying to pick and choose

Is the stock going to go up?

Is it going down?

When is it going up or down?

Which way is it going?
The reality is, nobody knows

Our goal is not to spend our time doing that

Our goal is to have our small businesses make us more money

And then have the profits automatically invested

The second way is to choose a mutual fund

Take those same stocks that are out there, and we pay a professional to pick them

The third is an index fund

An index fund is like the S&P 500

The S&P 500 is the 500 largest publicly traded companies in America that do business world wide

Nobody's picking and choosing

It's just the 500 largest companies

S&P stands for Standard and Poors

Many years ago, a publisher started tracking the 500 biggest companies

That companies name was Standard and Poors

The fourth is my favorite

Berkshire Hathaway

 Berkshire Hathaway is a stock

It's Warren Buffett's company,

It has its beginnings as a textile mill

The textile mill was not doing well so warren sold the assets and started investing them into other things

Mainly

Insurance

Its most well-known company is GEICO

They take the premiums and profits from the insurance companies and invest in other companies

They buy companies or stock in companies

For the vast majority of people

You should spend your time in step 1.

Making more money

Invest the profits into Berkshire Hathaway or S&P 500

Over a long period of time

Berkshire Hathaway has done better than the S&P 500

Mutual funds

And

Picking and choosing

One of the biggest reasons is the fees

Here are the plus and minuses of each

Picking and choosing the problem is, you're spending your time

You're spending your energy,
and
You don't know what's going on

The problem with pick and choose

Is that most people lose

A mutual fund is where you hire a professional manager, and they pick and choose the only negative to that is the fees that they're going to charge

So in this example, just to make it really simple, let's say that you got a 6% rate of return, and the fees were 2%

Most of the time you're never going to see the fee cost

It's in the small print

And the problem is that if you made 6%, and there's 2% in fees

Your profit is only 4% you just lost 33% of your investment by having somebody do that for you

The S&P 500

The reason we like it so much is that the fees are low

The fees are ½ of 1%

So in the same example, if it made a 6% rate of return minus the fees you would have 5.5%

And then the last one is Berkshire Hathaway

If you have that same 6% rate of return

The fees are about $5 in commission when you invest

If your stock made 6%

You get to keep all 6%

Because its a stock

Over time

Berkshire Hathaway has out performed

The S&P 500
Mutual funds
Picking and choosing

Berkshire is a conglomerate of many companies that they own or invested in

Those companies have gone up in value

They make money, and they take that money and reinvest it

That's why it's done so well

Mission #1 of the foundation

To provide financial rewards to students when they attend class and share with others

These rewards are to be added to their investment account

One of the missions of the foundation is to help you get started investing

That is why we giving away our Berkshire Hathaway stock

The foundation has give out over 30,000 financial rewards to students all over the world

We have over 3,000 students that have started saving and investing

To get a financial reward from the foundation go to

SuccessAndMoneyFoundation.Org

38

Warren Buffett
Berkshire Hathaway Stock

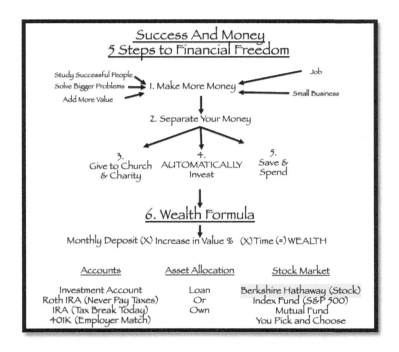

There is a wonderful book written by Robert Miles, called

101 Reasons to Own the World's Greatest Investment

Here are some of the reasons I like Berkshire Hathaway

One is a historic performance; it has outperformed many of the

Other mutual funds over a long period of time

Low cost, almost no cost, because there's no money under management, and it's got a proven track record

There is a wonderful owner's manual

Warren Buffett wants you to think like he does

Which is an owner of a business

It has a unique annual meeting

I've been at this meeting multiple times, and there's 40,000 people in the audience and hundreds of thousands of people watching online

There's no dividend

The problem is that with a dividend, they don't get a tax break, and you have to pay taxes on it at the highest rates

They've taken that money and reinvested it in their companies

There's no taxes on this until you sell it

So you can make it very easy to hand down from generation to generation

The chairman's age, he's been doing this for a long time, but more importantly, he's got a whole group of people that are trained that are going to take over when he retires

It acts like a mutual fund, but it does not have the same cost structure as a mutual fund

It has a unique charity program

It is a wonderful way to learn

He's a teacher, and warren said that when he passes away on his headstone, he wants to have the word 'teacher' written on it

Loyal shareholders

They're long-term holders

It's owner-managed

They have many companies that they purchased where the original owners are staying to manage it

It's got a stable portfolio, it's done really well on some of its tax exposure and asset protection

They reduced a lot of the investment mistakes

It's very easy for you to gift or to give away as an estate

Because it's a stock,

It's a smaller shareholder group

Business ownership

Investors have the ability to buy the stock in what they call a 'slice,' so you can buy it with any amount of money

Ownership

They focus on mergers and acquisitions

They like to write a check and buy things

They're investing with a higher purpose, the book value per share

We think that it's usually undervalued, which is a good thing

Equal opportunity investment,

Joining a winner,

Billionaire maker

Lots of people have made lots and lots of money owning this for the long term
So it does not have that movement up and down

It's outperformed the S&P 500 over a long period of time,

Which has outperformed mutual funds, which underperform

Pick-and-choose because when you pick and choose, you lose

Lower institutional ownership

It's included in the S&P

There's no tax return until you sell it

Small shareholders are welcome

You're buying a stock, but getting a lot of companies, similar to what you would in the S&P 500

It attracts the same kind of minds you're looking for, the same kind of people that think the same way that you do

It's not flashy

They're investing in things that are solid

They have great businesses that make money

A great way to allocate your assets

There is a large nonprofit foundation

Buffett's given away 99% of his money to charity

You think differently

You think like an owner, not like a speculator

You can give these gifts to the next generations, and it's very tax-efficient

Wonderful investment model and simplicity

So those are some great ideas of why we like Berkshire Hathaway

There are some great classes and interviews on Warren Buffett and Berkshire Hathaway

FREE Books and Classes

SuccessAndMoneyFoundation.Org/Books

SuccessAndMoneyFoundation.Org/Courses

39

Real Estate
Fix And Flip
And
Long Term Rentals

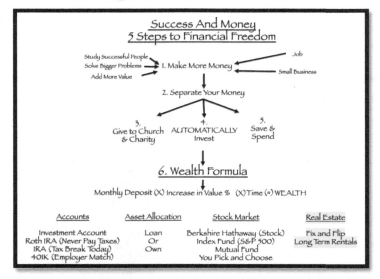

(Review Real Estate #s 16-21)

40

Save And Spend

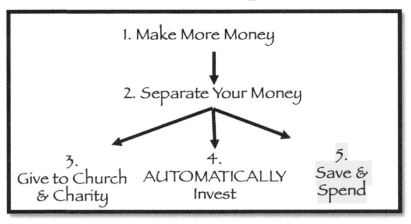

1. Make More Money

⬇

2. Separate Your Money

3.
Give to Church & Charity

4.
AUTOMATICALLY Invest

5.
Save & Spend

Where does all your money go?

- Auto, insurance, food, entertainment, credit cards, communication, medical, apparel
- Housing
- Taxes

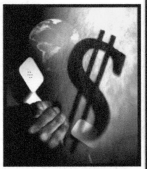

Most of the money that comes in is going to expenses, Your goal is to get it into long-term investments

This is how you reduce your expenses by 20% and invest the savings

Are there expenses that should or could go without?
Over a 40 year period with a 10% growth rate

$60 a month would grow to $350,000

$100 a month is $584,222

$400 a month is $2,336,888

$1,000 a month is $5,842,221

What are some other things that you're doing that you probably shouldn't?

The key is automatically invest 10%-20% of your income and let it grow

What do things really cost?

**Are you spending money on things
You could/should go without?**

Item	Cost	Times per month	Yearly cost	Same amount invested for 40 years @10%
Cigarettes	$ 4.00	15	$720	$350,533
Starbucks	$ 5.00	20	$1,200	$584,222
Alcohol	$100.00	4	$4,800	$2,336,888
Drugs	$250.00	4	$12,000	$5,842,221

41

Save 20%
When You Use Cash
Verses
A Debit Or Credit Card

Strategy: Cut up all personal credit cards, keep business cards.

- Carrying a credit card automatically increases your spending by 20%
- How much do you spend a month with your credit card?
  - **$3,000**
  - **$4,000**
  - **$5,000**

- Save a $600 to $1,000 with simple plastic surgery

42

Save by Switching Cards

 Cut Your Credit Card Expense

- What is the difference between these credit cards?
- About $300 a year in interest
- Are you tired of paying 18-21% on your credit cards when there are so many cards at 9% or less?

 Strategy: Pay Your Credit Card Debt in Half the Time

- Transfer your current high interest rate credit card to a lower interest rate credit card.
- Continue to pay the same payment and pay off the debt in half the time.

43

Increase Your Payments And Save

Credit Card Debt

- **$10,000** in credit card purchases
- Monthly payments of $183
- At that rate, it will take you 15 years to pay off the card
- You will have spent **$32,951**

Increase the payment from $183 to $395,
You will save $19,628

Increase your Credit Card Payments and Save

Loan Balance	%	Term Years	Payment	Total Interest	Grand Total	Difference
$ 1,000	21%	15.00	$ 18.31	$ 2,295	$ 3,295	
$ 1,000	21%	9.99	$ 20.00	$ 1,397	$ 2,397	$ 898
$ 1,000	21%	5.78	$ 25.00	$ 735	$ 1,735	$ 1,560
$ 1,000	21%	4.21	$ 30.00	$ 514	$ 1,514	$ 1,781
$ 1,000	21%	3.33	$ 35.00	$ 398	$ 1,398	$ 1,897
$ 1,000	21%	2.76	$ 40.00	$ 326	$ 1,326	$ 1,969
Loan Balance	%	Term Years	Payment	Total Interest	Grand Total	Difference
$ 10,000	21%	15.00	$ 183.06	$ 22,951	$ 32,951	
$ 10,000	21%	9.99	$ 200.00	$ 13,972	$ 23,972	$ 8,979
$ 10,000	21%	5.78	$ 250.00	$ 7,350	$ 17,350	$ 15,601
$ 10,000	21%	4.21	$ 300.00	$ 5,139	$ 15,139	$ 17,812
$ 10,000	21%	3.33	$ 350.00	$ 3,984	$ 13,984	$ 18,967
$ 10,000	21%	2.81	$ 395.00	$ 3,323	$ 13,323	$ 19,628

44

How The Banks Are Making 21%

And

Paying You Nothing

Millions of dollars are in checking and savings accounts making
1%
and millions of dollars are charged on credits cards at
21%

45

Getting Out Of Debt Summary

1. Make More Money

2. Don't Get Into Personal Debt

3. Switch To Cash Vs A Debit Card Or Credit Card

4. Fill Out and use The Cash Flow Tracker

5. Find Additional Money To Pay Off Credit Cards

6. Pay Off The Smallest Debt First

7. Take The Additional Money, Pay Off The Next Smallest Debt, Then The Next

46

How To Save Money On A Car

 Cut your Car Expenses by 20% to 50%

- Sticker Price — **$20,000**
- Hidden Costs
  - Paint/fabric protector
  - Undercoating
  - Dealer prep
  - Extended warranties
  - Credit life
  - Sales tax
  - Licensing fees
  - $6,500 in finance charges

- A $20,000 car becomes a **$30,000** decision

 Strategy: Buy a Late Model Used Car

- The day you buy a new car and drive it off the lot, it becomes a used car even before you get home
- Everyone drives a used car, but some people pay for a new one
- Buy a pre-owned vehicle
- A pre-owned is half the sticker price
- After finance charges, you save $15,000

47

How To Save Money On Insurance

-Insurance Review
-Eliminate Overlapping Insurance

Do An Insurance Review

Strategy: Do an Insurance review

- 13 Ways to reduce your insurance expenses by 20%
  - Eliminate overlapping coverage
  - Raise deductible
  - Buy term
  - Increase co-insurance amounts
  - Avoid some insurances completely

48

Save 20%-30% On Your Home

Save 20 to 30% on your own home

Your home is going to either be the best or worst financial decision

We're going to use the figure of $200,000 in this example

Now, depending on where you live in the world, you will either double it, triple it, or even 10 times it

The goal is to understand the concept and then multiply it

But a $200,000 house for 30 years

You're going to pay around $328,000 in interest

Plus $200,000 for the property

For a total of $528,000

For larger amounts, just add zeros or multiple each number, for example if you the average home is $500,000 (multiple each number by 2.5)

49

Buy Your Home For Less Money

-Write Offers

If there are 100 properties for sale, only 3-5% of them fit our criteria

The key to getting a good deal is to write offers, If you saved 10% on the purchase price

With reduced price and interest payments, you could save 10-15% of the total cost

On this $200,000 house you would save $52,830, a $500,000 house would be $52,830 x 2.5 = $132,075)

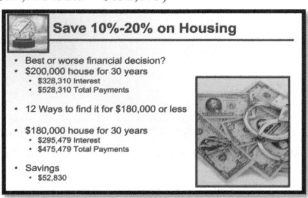

Save 10%-20% on Housing

- Best or worse financial decision?
- $200,000 house for 30 years
  - $328,310 Interest
  - $528,310 Total Payments

- 12 Ways to find it for $180,000 or less

- $180,000 house for 30 years
  - $295,479 Interest
  - $475,479 Total Payments

- Savings
  - $52,830

50

With Good Credit, You Can Reduce Your Interest Rate

-Pay Less Interest

Reduce Your Interest Rate

Loan Balance	$180,000	$180,000	$180,000
Interest Rate	8%	7%	6%
Term	30 years	30 years	30 years
Payment	$1,320	$1,197	$1,079
Total %	$295,479	$251,116	$208,508
Grand Total	$475,479	$431,116	$388,508
Difference		($44,363)	($86,971)
# of times item paid for	2.64	2.39	2.15

On a $500,00 home simply multiple by 2.5 (86,691 x 2.5 = $216,727)

51

Increase Your Monthly Payment And Pay Your House Off In Half The Time

By increasing you payment, you can pay your house off in half the time saving $115,099

On a $500,00 home simply multiple by 2.5 (115,099 x 2.5 = $287,747)

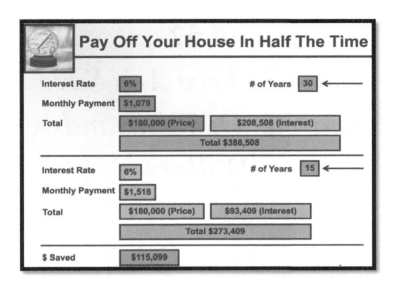

Pay Off Your House In Half The Time

	$180,000	$180,000	Difference
Loan Balance	$180,000	$180,000	**Difference**
Interest Rate	6%	6%	
Term	30 years	15 years	
Payment	$1,079	$1,518	$439
Total %	$208,508	$93,409	$115,099
Grand Total	$388,508	$273,409	
# of times item paid for	2.15	1.51	

52

Do All Three And Save Hundreds Of Thousands Of Dollars

-Lower Price
-Lower Interest
-Higher Payment

 Save 10%-20% on Housing

- BEFORE
- $200,000 house for 30 years
  - $328,310 Interest
  - $528,310 Total Payments

- AFTER
- Buy it for 180,000
- Reduce the Interest Rate
- Pay off the house in ½ the time

- Total Saved $254,900

Total saved $500,000 ($254,900 x 2.5 = $637,250)

53

Putting It All Together

Conservative investment plan, $100 a month for 20 years @10% rate of return = $372,490, not enough to beat inflation

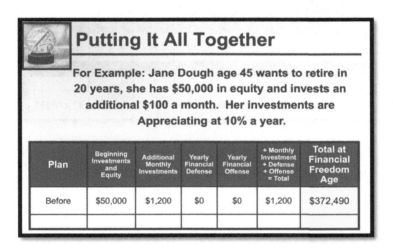

Putting It All Together

For Example: Jane Dough age 45 wants to retire in 20 years, she has $50,000 in equity and invests an additional $100 a month. Her investments are Appreciating at 10% a year.

Plan	Beginning Investments and Equity	Additional Monthly Investments	Yearly Financial Defense	Yearly Financial Offense	+ Monthly Investment + Defense + Offense = Total	Total at Financial Freedom Age
Before	$50,000	$1,200	$0	$0	$1,200	$372,490

Conservative Plan

In addition to our current plan, lets save an additional $200 a month in savings and start a small business and add an additional $1,200 a month to our investment account

Our new total is $1,477,388

Add Financial Defense and Offense

Plan	Beginning Investments and Equity	Additional Monthly Investments	Yearly Financial Defense	Yearly Financial Offense	+ Monthly Investment + Defense + Offense = Total	Total at Financial Freedom Age
Before	$50,000	$1,200	$0	$0	$1,200	$372,490
After						
Conservative	$50,000	$1,200	$2,400	$14,400	$18,000	$1,477,388

Realistic Plan

Lets increase our saving from $200 to $300 a month and increase business profits from $1,200 to $2,400 a month

Our new total is $2,503,269

Add Financial Defense and Offense

Plan	Beginning Investments and Equity	Additional Monthly Investments	Yearly Financial Defense	Yearly Financial Offense	+ Monthly Investment + Defense + Offense = Total	Total at Financial Freedom Age
Before	$50,000	$1,200	$0	$0	$1,200	$372,490
After						
Conservative	$50,000	$1,200	$2,400	$14,400	$18,000	$1,477,388
Realistic	$50,000	$1,200	$3,600	$28,800	$33,600	$2,503,269

Aggressive Plan

Lets increase our saving from $200 to $400 a month and increase business profits from $1,200 to $3,600 a month

Our new total is $4,476,211

Add Financial Defense and Offense

Plan	Beginning Investments and Equity	Additional Monthly Investments	Yearly Financial Defense	Yearly Financial Offense	+ Monthly Investment + Defense + Offense = Total	Total at Financial Freedom Age
Before	$50,000	$1,200	$0	$0	$1,200	$372,490
After						
Conservative	$50,000	$1,200	$2,400	$14,400	$18,000	$1,477,388
Realistic	$50,000	$1,200	$3,600	$28,800	$33,600	$2,503,269
Aggressive	$50,000	$1,200	$4,800	$57,600	$63,600	$4,476,211

This is what your balance sheet looks like

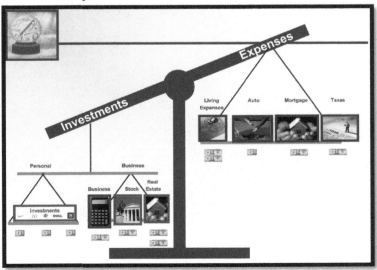

54

"Make A Difference

Make It Happen

Every Life Is Precious"

Thomas Painter

10 Post-Quiz Questions

1	**How much would you have if you put a $1 a day under your mattress for 66 years?** $24,090 or $41,458
2	**How much would you have if you invested a dollar a day at 3% for 66 years?** $38,686 or $75,736
3	**How much would you have if you invested a dollar a day at a 10% rate of return for 66 years?** $2,607,064 or $6,533,598
4	**How much would you owe if you charge a dollar a day on your credit card at 21% interest for 66 years?** $16,887,660 or $1,611,877,660
5	**If you used a credit card to buy a computer for $1,000 with 10 years of payments, How much would you pay in total?** $1,300 or $2,374
6	**With $1,000 in debt, After making payments for 4 years, How much do you still owe?** $325 or $771
7	**What is the Dow Stock Market Index?** 100 Companies from different industries or 30 Companies from different industries
8	**What is the S&P Stock Index?** 500 of the largest companies in America or 1,000 of the largest companies in America
9	**True of False, The S&P Stock Market Index makes more money than most professionally managed mutual funds?** True or False
10	**Berkshire Hathaway is a stock that is managed by Warren Buffett's team, over time, does it make more money that the S&P Stock index?** True or False

10 Pre-Quiz Answers

1	How much would you have if you put a $1 a day under your mattress for 66 years? $24,090
2	How much would you have if you invested a dollar a day at 3% for 66 years? $75,736
3	How much would you have if you invested a dollar a day at a 10% rate of return for 66 years? $2,607,064
4	How much would you owe if you charge a dollar a day on your credit card at 21% interest for 66 years? $1,611,877,660
5	If you used a credit card to buy a computer for $1,000 with 10 years of payments, How much would you pay in total? $2,374
6	With $1,000 in debt, After making payments for 4 years, How much do you still owe? $771
7	What is the Dow Stock Market Index? 30 Companies from different industries
8	What is the S&P Stock Index? 500 of the largest companies in America
9	True of False, The S&P Stock Market Index makes more money than most professionally managed mutual funds? True
10	Berkshire Hathaway is a stock that is managed by Warren Buffett's team, over time, does it make more money that the S&P Stock index? True
	How Many Questions Did You Get Right? Did You Do Better Than The Pre-Quiz?

Contact Us

If You Would Like To Help Us Share The Wealth Of Free
Success And Money Classes For Anyone, Anywhere

Please Email Me TPainter96@gmail.com

Thanks Tom Painter, Founder

For A FREE Membership
SuccessAndMoneyFoundation.org

Made in the USA
Las Vegas, NV
27 January 2024

84999422R00105